Nah! Nah! Nah!

A Comprehensive Teasing-Education Manual
For Grades 3 – 5

by
Richard L. Biren

Illustrated by
Harry Norcross

DEDICATION

To my daughter, Becca and my son, Jim.

ABOUT THE AUTHOR

Richard L. Biren is currently a certified elementary school counselor in Brush, Colorado. He has 20 years of experience at the elementary level. In addition, he has five years of experience as a counselor at the junior high/high school level in Minnesota and North Dakota and has taught at the community college level.

He holds BS and MS degrees from North Dakota State University and an Elementary Counselor Endorsement from Colorado State University. For the past 10 years, he has reviewed books as an NEA Professional Library Advisor.

In addition to teaching and counseling, Richard has written successful grant proposals for career education and bibliotherapy. He has also written articles published in regional counseling journals and newsletters.

Richard lives in Brush with his wife, Cindy, and their two children, Becca and Jim.

OTHER BOOKS BY RICHARD L. BIREN
PUBLISHED BY MAR*CO PRODUCTS, INC.

I Wonder Who (A Friendship-Skills Program)

Managing School Conflict

copyright © 1997
mar*co products, inc.

Published by
mar*co products, inc.
1443 Old York Road, Warminster, PA 18974
1-800-448-2197

Library of Congress Catalog Card Number: 96-079863

ISBN: 1-57543-020-7

Printed in the U.S.A.

TABLE OF CONTENTS

INTRODUCTION

This book is intended to help counselors and teachers deal with the ever-present problem of teasing. It is divided into three sections, making it easy for educators to focus on the aspects of teasing that are specific to for their situations.

It is not necessary to do every lesson. Facilitators may select any or all of the lessons in *Section 1—Teasing Awareness* and *Section 2—Dealing With Teasing*, and use those lessons as their curriculum. If *Section 3—Individual Planning* is to be presented, all of the material should be reproduced and distributed to the students.

The material in this book is designed for students in the middle elementary grades (3-5). The lessons not only provide students with basics to expand their knowledge and skills, but also require their active participation.

SECTION 1—TEASING AWARENESS

This section, which includes eight lessons, is intended to create and increase student awareness of teasing. While most students are familiar with teasing, they may not realize why students tease or understand the sensitive issues involved in most teasing or the feelings such behavior produces. Making students aware of such factors increases their understanding.

SECTION 2—DEALING WITH TEASING

This section includes ten lessons and provides a variety of ideas and techniques for dealing effectively with teasing. Students using these procedures will understand not only what to do, but how to do it. They will be prepared to handle most teasing.

SECTION 3—INDIVIDUAL PLANNING

This section includes information and worksheets. The material is meant to be used individually by students having trouble with teasing. It is important that all of the information and worksheets (pages 58-71) be reproduced and completed. Completing the entire program enables the student to examine the entire problem. If only one or two pages are completed, a student may miss an important concept. Skipping a page may lead to inappropriate and ineffective attempts to solve the problem.

Individual Planning works best if a counselor, teacher, or parent reviews the worksheets with the students. This practice permits feedback and an opportunity to provide helpful suggestions to students. It also helps the student remain focused on the topic.

Counselors or teachers creating their own units for classroom guidance or small-group counseling may find it helpful to survey the students either formally (questionnaire) or informally (oral questioning) as to their concerns about teasing. Knowing the students' abilities and interests can be valuable when selecting appropriate lessons and materials.

When teaching or counseling students about teasing, it is essential not to overlook the importance of support. Students who experience teasing difficulties often lack a positive self-concept and positive experiences. Because these students have experienced a great number of put-downs, they need positive interactions.

It is very important for a counselor or teacher to support students by maintaining a positive atmosphere in the classroom or small-group setting. This is done by establishing rules when the class or group first meets, enforcing them consistently, and recognizing those who abide by them.

Encourage students to use what they have learned. Make a practice of complimenting students for their efforts. Compliments help students get along with each other and improve the school climate. They also can make the tasks of teaching and learning more enjoyable and successful.

When teaching, it is important to make sure that students have grasped the information and ideas presented to them. If students have difficulty grasping an idea or technique, break it into smaller parts or model it to show what needs to be done. *Contrast* is another helpful technique. For example, if you are talking about assertive actions, stare down at your feet, mumble, pinch your shoulders inward, and make your voice sound scared. This will get everyone's attention. It also provides a teachable moment when you can demonstrate proper behavior. Students will understand what you are doing and realize what is needed.

Finally, remember that despite your best efforts, situations will arise that require outside help. If you find teasing escalating beyond what a student can handle, make additional help available. You may need to involve your administrator, parents, outside agencies such as a mental health clinic, law enforcement, or some other resource to help the student deal effectively with the difficulty. Be aware of your limits and always act in the best interest of the student.

SECTION 1
TEASING AWARENESS

LESSON 1
TEASING IN MY LIFE

Purpose:

To help students understand the meaning of teasing and become more aware of teasing at home and in school.

Materials Needed:

For each student: Copy of *Home/School* (page 9), pencil, crayons, and/or markers

For each leader: Suggested definition of *teasing:* To pester or irritate by saying or doing annoying or mean things. To joke or make good-humored fun about a person.

Activity:

The leader should:

- Introduce him/herself and any students not acquainted with the class or group.

- Give each student a *Home/School* worksheet, pencils, markers, and/or crayons.

- In the *Home* section, ask the students to draw a picture of a teasing situation they have experienced in their homes or in their neighborhoods. Tell them they will have five minutes to complete the task. Tell the students that they may use stick figures to illustrate what is happening in the picture.

  Variation: Those who wish to write a short description or story instead of drawing a picture should be allowed to do so. Tell the students not to use names in their writings or drawings.

- Ask the students to follow the same directions and complete the *School* section of the worksheet. Allow five minutes for this activity.

- Have each student share one of the experiences on his/her worksheet. Remind the students to describe what happened without using any names. When sharing, ask the students to describe their situation without putting anyone down.

- Ask the students to complete the following sentence stem on the back of the worksheet.

     Teasing is... (Allow three minutes for the students to complete the sentence.)

- Ask for volunteers to share their sentences.

- Conclude the lesson by sharing with the group your definition of *teasing.* (Definition found on page 11.)

8

NAH! NAH! NAH!

HOME/SCHOOL

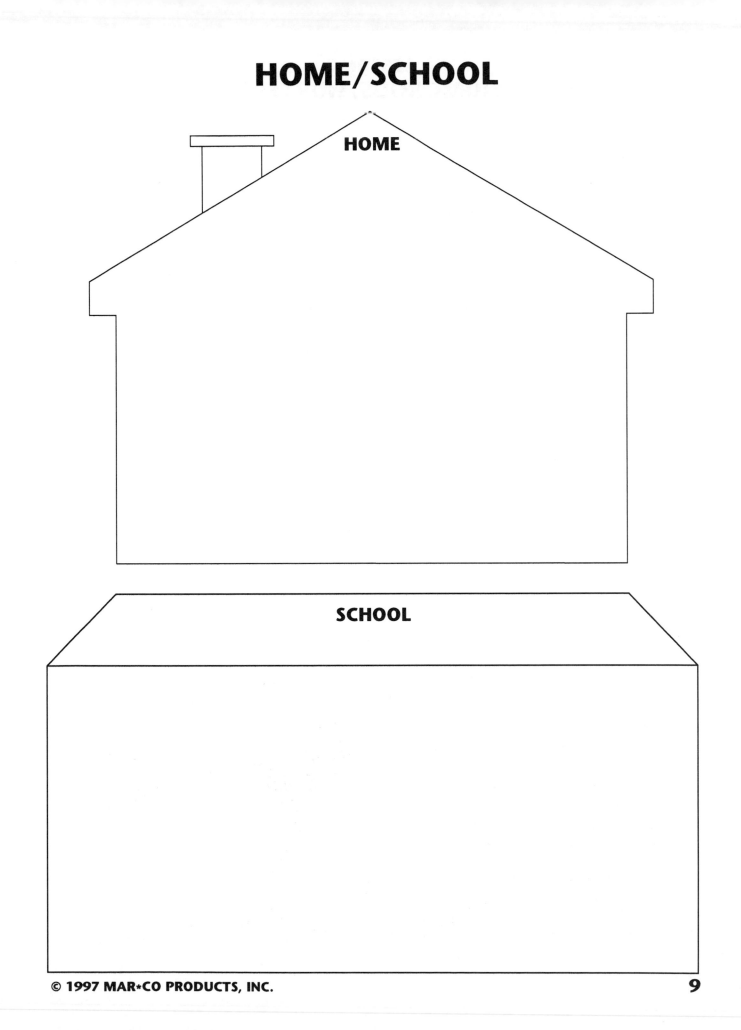

HOME

SCHOOL

LESSON 2
HUMOROUS/HURTFUL

Purpose:

To increase student awareness of the difference between two kinds of teasing: friendly/humorous and unfriendly/hurtful.

Materials Needed:

For each pair of students: Copy of *Role-Play Starters* (page 13)

For each leader: Copy of *Teasing Information* (page 11) and *Teasing Behavior Chart* (page 12)

Activity:

The leader should:

- Review with the students the *Teasing Information* sheet and the *Teasing Behavior Chart.* Emphasize that it is not so much what a person does, but the feeling(s) his/her actions create that determine whether teasing is humorous or hurtful.

- Divide the students into pairs. Assign one student in each pair to be Partner 1 and the other student to be Partner 2. Give each pair of students a copy of the *Role-Play Starters*. Ask them to role-play each situation twice. The first role-play should demonstrate teasing in a hurtful manner. Repeat the same role-play, but tease in a friendly, humorous manner. Tell the students that if they are not sure whether teasing is humorous or hurtful, they can decide by asking themselves: "Would I enjoy having someone do this to me?" If the answer is "yes," then the teasing is probably friendly or humorous.

- Ask each pair, if time permits, to select one role-play to perform for the entire group. First, role-play the situation as friendly. Then repeat the role-play as unfriendly. After each pair of students has role-played its situation both ways, ask: "What is the difference between friendly/humorous and unfriendly/hurtful teasing?" (If the students cannot find a difference, ask them to suggest what could be done to change the situations to make the differences easier to identify.)

  Variation: Have each group role-play a situation. Have the rest of the students try to guess whether the teasing is humorous or hurtful.

- Conclude the lesson by reinforcing the difference between humorous and hurtful teasing.

TEASING INFORMATION

General:

What is Teasing? *Teasing* is when someone repeatedly annoys or irritates another person with words or actions.

Kinds of Teasing:

A. Friendly/Humorous—this occurs when the teasing makes everyone involved, including the person being teased, laugh/smile at the situation.

B. Unfriendly/Hurtful—this occurs when the teasing makes everyone laugh/smile at the person being teased but the person being teased feels uncomfortable or hurt.

Examples:

When a parent strokes his/her fingers across the bottom of a child's foot to make the child laugh. (TYPE A)

When someone says, "Tattletale! Tattletale! You're always running to the teacher." The other person yells angrily, "That's not true! I don't always do it." (TYPE B)

When someone shouts, "Have it your way! You're nothing but a baby! Always have to have it your way." The other person stares at the floor. (TYPE B)

When someone smiles and says, "You know which way to go?" The other person, who made a basket in the wrong hoop, laughs and says, "Sure." (TYPE A)

When someone makes a threatening gesture and the other person bursts into tears. (TYPE B)

When someone calls, "Hey, Fatso!" The fat person yells angrily, "I am not!" (TYPE B)

When someone big drops his/her books on the floor and another person says, "Hey, Klutz, do you need a wheelbarrow?" The person who dropped the books smiles and replies jokingly, "I must, I can't believe I did that!" (TYPE A)

When someone shouts, "Stupid Carl, he can't play ball." Carl grits his teeth, clenches his fist, and screams, "What do you know?" (TYPE B)

TEASING BEHAVIOR CHART

KINDS OF TEASING

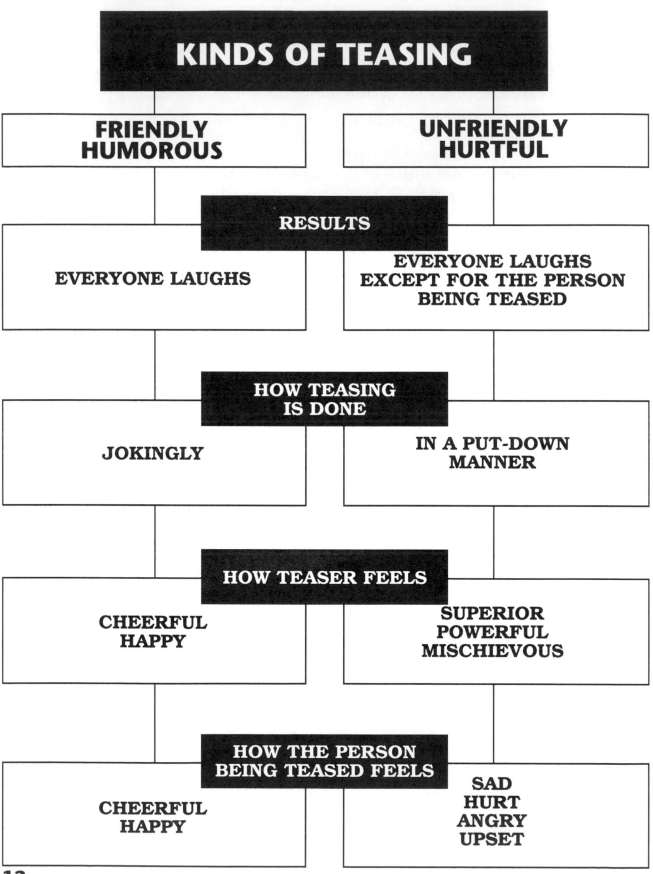

FRIENDLY HUMOROUS	UNFRIENDLY HURTFUL
RESULTS	
EVERYONE LAUGHS	EVERYONE LAUGHS EXCEPT FOR THE PERSON BEING TEASED
HOW TEASING IS DONE	
JOKINGLY	IN A PUT-DOWN MANNER
HOW TEASER FEELS	
CHEERFUL HAPPY	SUPERIOR POWERFUL MISCHIEVOUS
HOW THE PERSON BEING TEASED FEELS	
CHEERFUL HAPPY	SAD HURT ANGRY UPSET

NAH! NAH! NAH!

ROLE-PLAY STARTERS

The following situations are intended to be used as starters. You may add or subtract from each to show humorous or hurtful teasing. Remember, try to role-play each situation with your partner both ways. You may change what you say, how you say things, gestures, posture, and facial expressions to create humorous and hurtful situations.

PARTNER 1: You have just finished giving an oral report to the class

PARTNER 2: Say: "That was good."

PARTNER 2: You spill your tray at lunch.

PARTNER 1: Say: "You need help."

PARTNER 2: You are wearing a new shirt.

PARTNER 1: Say: "Where did you get that shirt?"

PARTNER 2: You make a mistake when competing on the Knowledge Bowl Team.

PARTNER 1: Say: "What were you thinking?"

PARTNER 1: You sneak up behind Partner 2, tap him/her on the back of the left shoulder, and quickly move to his/her right side.

PARTNER 2: You turn to your left and see nothing.

LESSON 3
TARGETS FOR TEASING

Purpose:

To increase student awareness of the reasons why people tease others.

Materials Needed:

For each student: Copy of the blank *Cartoon Worksheet* (page 16), pencil

For the leader: Transparency of *Sensitive Issues Chart* (page 15) and overhead projector or *Sensitive Issues Chart* (page 15) written on chalkboard or whiteboard

Activity:

The leader should:

- Give each student a blank *Cartoon Worksheet* and a pencil. Tell the students to complete the cartoon bubbles by writing what each character might say if one were teasing the other. Allow 3-5 minutes for this activity.

- When the allotted time has elapsed, have the students turn their papers face down.

- Use the overhead projector or board to review the *Sensitive Issues Chart.* Ask the students to give examples of each issue as it is mentioned. If the students are unable to give an example of a particular issue, the leader should supply one.

- Reread the issues on the *Sensitive Issues Chart.* After each entry is read, ask the students to raise their hands if they depicted that issue in one of their cartoons.

- Ask the students who did not raise their hands to describe issues their cartoon(s) illustrated. Allow time for the group to share. Add any new issues to the *Sensitive Issues Chart.*

- Conclude the lesson by summarizing the sensitive issues that have been discussed.

SENSITIVE ISSUES CHART

ISSUE	TEASING ACTION WORD(S)/GESTURE(S)
Physical Feature: Weight Height Vision Unusual Body Part	 Skinny, Fatso, Exaggerate walk/looks Shorty, Tree Four-eyes, Nerd Bug-eyes, Weirdo, Freak
Challenged: Mentally Physically	 Mental, Stupid, Idiot, Retard, Index finger pointed towards side of head with finger moved in circular motion Spastic, Mocking gestures of their actions (walk, talk)
Intelligence:	Bookworm, Nerd, Geek, Brain, Curve-raiser
Race:	Nigger, Honky, Boy, Whitey, Wetback
Social:	Mocking gestures, Pretend it's harmful to get too close to such a person, Make fun of where they live or what they wear

CARTOON WORKSHEET

NAH! NAH! NAH!

LESSON 4
HOW DO OTHERS REACT TO TEASING?

Note:

Lesson 4 should be used with Lesson 5.

Purpose:

To increase student awareness of how people react to teasing.

Materials Needed:

For each student: 2 copies (2 observations per page) of *Teasing Observation Form* (page 18), pencil

Activity:

The leader should:

- Give each student four copies of the *Teasing Observation Form.* Explain how each form should be completed.

- Give an example of teasing and ask for volunteers to role-play the situation. Before the role-play begins, ask the students to observe the role-play carefully. When it is finished, ask the students to complete a *Teasing Observation Form.*

- Check each observation for accuracy. Correct any errors by explaining what the correct answer might be.

- If you think that some students did not understand the instructions for completing the forms or the role-play, repeat the role-play activity. It is important that every student is comfortable with the form and understands how to complete it.

- Conclude the lesson by assigning each student the task of completing three observations independently before the next meeting of the group or class. The students should bring their completed *Teasing Observation Forms* with them to the next meeting.

TEASING OBSERVATION FORM

Place _____

Date _____ Time _____

Describe what happened:

_____

_____

_____

Who was there?

_____

_____

Why was the teasing done?

_____

_____

_____

TEASING OBSERVATION FORM

Place _____

Date _____ Time _____

Describe what happened:

_____

_____

_____

Who was there?

_____

_____

Why was the teasing done?

_____

_____

_____

LESSON 5
TEASING REACTIONS

Note:

Lesson 5 should be used with Lesson 4.

Purpose:

To increase student awareness of how people look and act when they are being teased.

Materials Needed:

For each student: Completed *Teasing Observation Forms* from Lesson 4, blank sheet of paper, pencil, and crayons or markers

For the leader: Copy of *Non-Verbal Communications* (page 20); overhead projector, transparency and transparency marker, whiteboard and dry erase marker, or chalkboard and chalk

Activity:

The leader should:

- Ask the students to look at their completed *Teasing Observation Forms*. Ask for volunteers to share what they observed. Allow time for every student who wishes to do so to share at least one observation.

- Review the information on *Non-Verbal Communications*. Discuss gestures, posture, and facial expressions. Tell the students what each is and how each communicates.

- Give each student a blank sheet of paper, pencil, and crayons or markers. Tell the students to draw a picture of someone being teased. Remind the students to show posture, facial expression, and gesture(s). Set a time limit for the activity.

- Have the students share their drawings with the class or group.

- Use an overhead projector, whiteboard, or chalkboard to create a list of body postures, gestures, and facial expressions associated with teasing. Ask the students to contribute their ideas to the list.

- Conclude the lesson by summarizing the lists.

NON-VERBAL COMMUNICATIONS

1. *Gesture* is the deliberate movement of a body part or limb.

   EXAMPLES:

Movement	Communicates
Pinch nose	Disgust
Clap hands	Approval
Clench fist	Anger
Tap shoulder	Desire for attention
Place finger over lips	Silence
Stick tongue out	Dislike

2. *Posture* is the body position a person holds. Whether you're sitting or standing, posture refers to how you position your body's trunk and your head, arms, legs, hands, and feet.

   EXAMPLES:

Position	Communicates
Standing with head down, eyes staring at ground	Lack of confidence Tiredness
Standing with head up, making eye contact with others	Pride Positive self-image
Sitting with arms folded and legs crossed	Unwillingness to cooperate Irritation
Sitting with head up and feet on floor.	Alertness Readiness

3. *Facial expression* is how you position your mouth and eyes/eyebrows.

   EXAMPLES:

Position	Communicates
Corners of mouth up, eyes open	Happiness
Mouth opened wide, eyes opened wide like saucers	Fear Surprise
Mouth pinched shut, eyebrows squeezed together, eyes narrowed	Anger
Corners of mouth down, eyes staring downward	Sadness Embarrassment

LESSON 6
FEELINGS AND TEASING

Purpose:

To increase student awareness of how people feel when they are teased.

Materials Needed:

For each student: Blank sheet of lined paper and pencil

For the leader: Copy of *Dear Teaser Letter* (page 22); overhead projector, transparency and transparency marker, whiteboard and dry erase marker, or chalkboard and chalk

Activity:

The leader should:

- Read the *Dear Teaser Letter* aloud to the students.

- Ask the students to think about a time when they were teased or saw someone being teased. Give each student paper and a pencil. Tell the students to write a make-believe letter to the person who did the teasing. The letters should express how the students felt or would have felt if they were teased in this manner. Remind the students not to use names of real people in their letters. Give the students 10-15 minutes to complete this activity.

- Ask the students to share their letters with the class or group. As the letters are read, write the different feelings expressed by the students on the overhead projector or board. (These feelings may include fear, anger, frustration, worry, sadness, embarrassment, helplessness, etc.)

- Conclude the lesson by summarizing the feelings listed.

DEAR TEASER LETTER

February 1, 1997

Dear Teaser,

I want you to know how much I hate it when you make fun of the way I talk. I can't help it if I can't say certain sounds. I work with the speech clinician daily, but I still have trouble. It's not fair for you to embarrass me by imitating the way I talk.

Would you please stop?

Sincerely,

Jamie Jones

LESSON 7
REACTING TO TEASING

Purpose:

To increase student awareness of how people act when they are teased.

Materials Needed:

For each pair of students: Copy of *Reaction Sheet* (page 24), copy of *Tease Sheet* (page 25), 2 pairs of scissors

For the leader: Overhead projector and transparency marker, whiteboard and dry erase marker, or chalkboard and chalk

Activity:

The leader should:

- Divide the students into pairs. Give each student a pair of scissors. Give one member of each pair a *Reaction Sheet*. Give their partner a *Tease Sheet*. Have the students cut along the lines to make individual slips. Make separate piles for *teases* and *reactions*. Place the slips face down. Shuffle each pile.

- Have the partners choose one member of each pair to act out the reactions and one to act out the teasing. Have each partner draw a slip from the appropriate pile. Then have each student role-play what is on his/her slip. The teaser should go first.

- Have the partners switch roles. The *teaser* now becomes the *reactor* and the *reactor* becomes the *teaser*. Have each partner draw a slip from the appropriate pile and enact the next role-play.

- Have the students continue role-playing and switching roles after each enactment until they have performed all the role-plays.

- Ask the students to think about times when they have been teased or when they teased others. Then ask them to answer the question: "How do people act when they are teased?" Write their answers on the overhead projector or board.

- Conclude the lesson by orally summarizing what is written on the overhead projector or board.

REACTION SHEET

You turn red and look like you are ready to explode with anger.	You mumble to yourself, look at the ground, and turn red.
You burst into tears.	You scream, "No! No! No! No!"
You stare at your feet.	You tell on him/her.
You say, "You're dumb. Only a dummy would do that!"	You smile.
You shake your closed fists back and forth.	You walk away.

NAH! NAH! NAH!

TEASE SHEET

Setting: Your partner asks your teacher if there was homework.

You whisper: "You idiot. She just told us there wasn't any homework."

Setting: Your partner is the pitcher of the opposing team. He/She can't pitch the ball over the plate.

You say: "You throw like an old lady."

Setting: Your partner has been told he/she is not allowed to go to a friend's house.

You say: "You're not allowed to go! Throw a tantrum, you'll get your way."

Setting: Yesterday, you saw your partner talking to your teacher. Today, you walk past him/her in the hall.

You say: "Teacher's Pet! Teacher's Pet!

Setting: You see your partner in the hallway showing his/her pictures.

You point, twist your face, shake your head disapprovingly.

Setting: Your partner comes to school with a short hair cut.

You say: "Looks like someone got too close to the mower."

Setting: Your partner is walking down the street.

You say: "Hey weirdo, where did you get those clothes? The dump?"

Setting: Your partner refuses to try to clear the big ramp on his/her skateboard.

You say: "What's wrong? Chicken?"

Setting: You hear the music your partner is listening to.

You say: "You must be a freak to listen to that stuff."

Setting: You spot your partner wearing a new hat. You grab it and toss it to a buddy.

You say, "Let's play *Keep Away*."

LESSON 8
WHY PEOPLE TEASE

Purpose:

To increase student awareness of the reasons why people tease others.

Materials Needed:

For each student: Copy of *Reasons For Teasing* (page 28), pencil

For the leader: Copy of *Why Students Tease* (page 27)

Activity:

The leader should:

* Read the *Why Students Tease* information to the students. Ask the students to give examples of each reason as it is named. Remind the students not to use people's names when giving their examples.

* Give each student a copy of *Reasons For Teasing* and a pencil. Ask the students to match each situation with a reason. Set a time limit for this activity.

* Have the students read their answers and correct their papers. Emphasize that it is sometimes difficult to tell why someone is teasing and sometimes there is more than one reason why someone teases.

   For example, Cliff stares at Raul and asks, "What did you say?" Cliff may be seeking revenge because Raul accidentally pushed him. At the same time, Cliff gains power by demanding, in a teasing manner, that Raul apologize to him.

* Conclude the lesson by summarizing the reasons why students tease.

REASONS FOR TEASING

Directions: Match the reason in the first column to the situation in the second column by writing the letter in the box. There is only one right answer for each item.

REASON	SITUATION
1. **C** Attention	A. Geraldine cries whenever Harold teases her about her hair. Harold tells his friends he can make her cry whenever he wants.
2. **G** Model	B. Maggie is constantly teasing her sister about being a perfect angel. Maggie is constantly hearing from her dad, "You're terrible. You're mean!"
3. **A** Power	C. Billy is home by himself most of the time. At school, he constantly teases everyone. His teacher has little time to attend to others because of Billy's teasing.
4. **F** Insecurity	D. Sheila hangs out with a group of girls who dislike Betty. When Sheila sees Betty, she says, "Where did you get those ugly clothes? The local swap shop?"
5. **B** Expectation	E. Last year, Hank spilled milk on Frank's baseball cards. Whenever Frank sees Hank, he laughs, points, and chants, "There goes the Klutz! There goes the Klutz!"
6. **D** Belonging	F. Olgama doesn't do well in school. Whenever anyone receives an award or is recognized for good work, Olgama blurts, "Cheater! Cheater!"
7. **E** Revenge	G. At home, Carlos is constantly teased about being a nerd. At school, Carlos teases by pointing and saying, "Look at the Nerd!"

28   NAH! NAH! NAH!

WHY STUDENTS TEASE

1. MODEL

Some students have been teased by others. They mimic what has happened to them by doing the same thing to others.

2. INSECURITY

Some students put others down by teasing. They believe this allows them to look superior. When they think they look superior, they don't feel so insecure.

3. REVENGE

Some students tease as a way of getting even with those who hurt or irritate them.

4. BELONGING

Some students tease in order to be part of a group. They feel that by teasing people the group members dislike, they will be looked upon with favor by group members.

5. ATTENTION

Some students tease to get others to pay attention to them.

6. EXPECTATIONS

Some students have significant others (parents, brothers, sisters) who constantly tell them they are bad. They are told, "You can't do anything right," or "You're terrible." These students live up to these negative expectations by teasing others.

7. POWER

Some students tease in order to control others. They feel in control when their teasing causes others to react in certain ways.

REASONS FOR TEASING

Directions: Match the reason in the first column to the situation in the second column by writing the letter in the box. There is only one right answer for each item.

REASON

SITUATION

1. ☐ Attention

A. Geraldine cries whenever Harold teases her about her hair. Harold tells his friends he can make her cry whenever he wants.

2. ☐ Model

B. Maggie is constantly teasing her sister about being a perfect angel. Maggie is constantly hearing from her dad, "You're terrible. You're mean!"

3. ☐ Power

C. Billy is home by himself most of the time. At school, he constantly teases everyone. His teacher has little time to attend to others because of Billy's teasing.

4. ☐ Insecurity

D. Sheila hangs out with a group of girls who dislike Betty. When Sheila sees Betty, she says, "Where did you get those ugly clothes? The local swap shop?"

5. ☐ Expectation

E. Last year, Hank spilled milk on Frank's baseball cards. Whenever Frank sees Hank, he laughs, points, and chants, "There goes the Klutz! There goes the Klutz!"

6. ☐ Belonging

F. Olgama doesn't do well in school. Whenever anyone receives an award or is recognized for good work, Olgama blurts, "Cheater! Cheater!"

7. ☐ Revenge

G. At home, Carlos is constantly teased about being a nerd. At school, Carlos teases by pointing and saying, "Look at the Nerd!"

SECTION 2
DEALING WITH TEASING

LESSON 1
DEALING WITH A TEASER

Purpose:

To help students learn to prepare to deal with a teaser.

Materials Needed:

For each student: Copy of *Assertive Actions* (page 31), *Assertive Action Observation Worksheet* (page 32), pencil

For the leader: Copy of *Assertive Actions* (page 31), *Assertive Action Observation Worksheet* (page 32)

Activity:

The leader should:

- Give each student a copy of *Assertive Actions* and *Assertive Action Observation Worksheet*. Review the information with the students. Answer any questions the students may have.

- Divide the students into pairs. Tell each pair to create a teasing situation in which one partner will play the part of the person who teases and the other partner will be the person being teased. The person being teased will practice assertive actions.

- Have the pair role-play the situation. When the role-play is finished, have the partner being teased talk to the partner doing the teasing about what has just happened. The partner who was doing the teasing should then complete the *Assertive Action Observation Worksheet*. When they have finished, the partners should discuss what was written.

- Have the partners switch roles and repeat the activity.

- Ask the group: "What is the most important action a person being teased should do when talking to the person who is doing the teasing?" Allow time for answers.

- Ask the students to choose what they believe is the most important action on the *Assertive Action Observation Worksheet*. Read each action and tell the students to raise their hands when their choice is read.

- Conclude the lesson by summarizing and emphasizing all of the assertive actions mentioned.

ASSERTIVE ACTIC

In dealing with a teaser, it is important to us
Assertive actions show that you respect you
tions tell the teaser that you are willing to sta
Knowing that you have the confidence to d
teaser to think twice about continuing the tea

ACTIONS

1. Make frequent direct eye contact while talking and listening.
2. Listen carefully. Be quiet and remember what is said.
3. Speak clearly. Use polite words and tone of voice.
4. Face the person teasing you.
5. Say exactly what you want to say.

PREPARATION

Before using assertive actions, it is helpful to:

1. Think about what you can do to stop the teasing.
2. Believe that you can stop the teasing.
3. Use positive self-talk: Say to yourself, "I know I can do it."
4. Practice what you will say and how you will act. Practice in front of a mirror or with a friend.

ASSERTIVE ACTION OBSERVATION WORKSHEET

TEASER _____

PERSON BEING TEASED _____

Directions: Place a check (✓) in front of each action your partner used while talking to you about your teasing.

☐ 1. Made direct eye contact often.

☐ 2. Appeared to listen.

☐ 3. Was quiet.

☐ 4. Spoke clearly.

☐ 5. Used polite words.

☐ 6. Faced me.

☐ 7. Talked to me about the teasing.

LESSON 2
THE "I" MESSAGE

Purpose:

To increase student awareness of what "I" Messages are and how to use them.

Materials Needed:

For each student: Copy of *"I" Message Construction* (page 34), *"I" Message* poster (page 35), *"I" Message Worksheet* (page 36), pencil

For the leader: Copy of *"I" Message Construction* (page 34), *"I" Message* poster (page 35), *"I" Message Worksheet* (page 36)

Activity:

The leader should:

- Give each student a copy of *"I" Message Construction.* Review the information with the students and provide some examples. Answer any questions the students may have.

- Give each student an *"I" Message* poster to complete. When the students have finished, ask them to share their responses. Check their answers for accuracy.

- Give each student a copy of the *"I" Message Worksheet.* Complete the first situation as a group. Then ask each student to individually construct an "I" Message for each of the remaining situations. Set a time limit for completing the activity.

- Ask for volunteers to share their answers with the class or group. Compliment the good responses and correct any errors by asking the other students for suggestions for improvement. If necessary, review the specific components of the "I" Message, asking if each part is included in the student's statement.

- Ask for volunteers to role-play a teasing situation in front of the group. Tell the students performing the role-play to use an "I" Message.

- Conclude the lesson by having the students orally respond to the following sentence stem:

    "I" Messages can help me when I am being teased because..."

"I" MESSAGE CONSTRUCTION

An "I" Message is made up of three parts.

The first part tells others how you feel. For example, you might say, "I feel angry." This lets others know how you feel about a situation. By saying it, you share your feelings. This information can be helpful to others who may not understand your feelings.

The second part tells others what caused you to feel the way you do. For example, you could say, "I feel angry when you throw my cap on the floor." This "I" Message not only lets others know how you feel, but also tells them why you feel that way. After hearing this part of your "I" Message they know what caused you to have these feelings. The person who threw your cap now knows he/she is responsible for the way you feel.

In the third part, you ask others to act differently. You suggest what they can do to help the situation. For example, you might say, "I feel angry when you throw my cap on the floor. Please don't do that!" In the last sentence, you offer a solution without making a demand. The person doing the teasing now has a choice to make.

By using an "I" Message, you hope to stop the teasing. For those who are unaware of how their teasing makes you feel, giving an "I" Message may help bring about change. An "I" Message can solve the problem.

I FEEL

Express how you feel—angry, irritated, sad, annoyed, hurt, etc.

WHEN

Indicate what action(s) have caused you to feel the way you do.

PLEASE

Indicate what you want. Sometimes it's nothing more than asking the person who is doing the teasing to stop doing it.

"I" Message

I feel _____

when _____

_____

_____

_____

Please _____

_____

_____

_____

"I" MESSAGE WORKSHEET

Directions: For each teasing situation, fill in the blanks with an "I" Message. We will complete the first answer as a group, and you will do the rest on your own.

1. You are outside on the playground when Jorge grabs your cap and runs off, saying, "Thanks for the cap." He looks back, expecting you to run after him.

    *I feel*_____
    when _____ .
    Please _____
    _____ .

2. You approach a group of students who are examining a piece of paper. As you look, Patricia grabs the paper, puts it in her pocket, twists her face, and says sarcastically, "Monkeys always look!"

    *I feel*_____
    when _____ .
    Would you _____
    _____ ?

3. You're sitting at your desk working on your math test. Thor whispers, "Remember, you're dumb. Put down the wrong answers. You'll make the rest of us look good."

    *I feel*_____
    when _____ .
    *I would appreciate it if you*_____
    _____ .

4. The ball rolls through your legs into the outfield. Harry yells from the dugout, "Way to go, Steve! I'm glad you're not on my team."

    *I feel*_____
    when _____ .
    Please _____
    _____ .

LESSON 3
APOLOGIZING

Purpose:

To increase student awareness about actions that may result in others teasing them and to practice apologizing.

Materials Needed:

For each student: Copy of *Annoying Habits* (page 38)

For the leader: None

Activity:

The leader should:

- Ask the students to think about students who have annoying mannerisms. (For example, picking nose, clicking teeth, slurping food, tapping fingers, etc.) Allow time for the students to think.

- Say to the students, "Please raise your hand if you have ever felt like teasing a person about an annoying habit."

- Then ask, "Suppose you were the one with the annoying habit and someone teased you. What could you do?" Allow the students time to share their ideas with the class or group. Then ask, "Would apologizing solve the problem?" Allow time for the students to answer.

- Give each student a copy of *Annoying Habits*. Direct the students to divide into pairs. Tell the students to use the list of annoying habits and take turns modeling the annoying action and teasing the other person. When the teasing occurs, the partner modeling the annoying habit should apologize. For example, he/she should say, "I'm sorry. I didn't realize that bothered you. I won't do it again." Allow enough time for the students to complete several of the annoying-habit situations.

- Conclude the lesson by telling the students that apologizing is one way of dealing effectively with teasing when they themselves are part of the problem. However, apologizing is *not* appropriate if they have done nothing wrong.

ANNOYING HABITS

UNCLEAN HANDS/FACE

LAUGHING IN A WEIRD WAY

SNORTING

PICKING NOSE

SCRATCHING HABITS

WHISTLING

TAPPING FINGERS

SPITTING

SLURPING

STICKING OUT TONGUE

STARING

MUMBLING

TWIRLING HAIR

SLOPPY DRESSING

GOSSIPING

THROWING TANTRUMS

LYING

STEALING

POUTING

SWEARING

CHEATING

WIPING MOUTH ON SLEEVE AFTER EATING/DRINKING

NAH! NAH! NAH!

LESSON 4
COMPLIMENTS

Purpose:

To increase student awareness of how compliments can be used to deal with teasing and provide students with practice in giving compliments.

Materials Needed:

For each student: Copy of *Kindness, Spread It Around* poster (page 41)

For the leader: Whiteboard and dry erase marker, chalkboard and chalk, or over-head projector, transparency, and transparency marker; the following rules for giving and receiving compliments written on the board or transparency.

When you are giving a compliment:

1. Make eye contact with the person to whom you are giving the compliment.
2. Use a pleasant voice.
3. State what you like about the person.

When you are receiving a compliment:

1. Make eye contact with the person who is giving you the compliment.
2. Use a pleasant voice.
3. Say "Thanks" or "Thank you."

Activity:

The leader should:

- Ask the students to define the word *compliment*. Allow time for responses. When the students have finished, tell them that a compliment is a positive statement about how someone looks or acts.

- Give some compliments to the students. Go around the group and make statements like: "You listen well." "I like your hair." "Your shirt looks beautiful." or "You do great work."

- Ask the students if they know what to do when they want to give someone a compliment. Allow time for responses. After several students have responded, go over the rules for giving and receiving compliments. These rules should be written on the board or shown on the overhead projector. (When reviewing the rules, you may wish to show incorrect actions—such as looking away, using an angry voice, and denying the compliment—and then show the correct actions.)

- Tell the students to divide into pairs and practice giving compliments to each other. Allow 2-3 minutes for this activity.

- Divide the students into two equal teams. Have one team form a line on one side of the room. Have the other team stand in a line on the other side of the room. Tell the students that they are going to have a "Compliment Down." This means that each student, in turn, must follow the proper actions for giving and receiving a compliment. Any student not following the proper actions within 15 seconds will go back to his/her seat. Explain that the game will start with the first person on Team 1 giving a compliment to the first person on Team 2. The first person on Team 2 will then give a compliment to the second person on Team 1. The second person on Team 1 will give a compliment to the second person on Team 2. Compliments will continue until the last person is reached. Before beginning the game, answer any questions the students may have about how the game is played.

- Give each student a copy of the *Kindness, Spread It Around* poster. Discuss with the students the meaning of the statement written on the poster. Instruct each student to write his/her name in the center circle. Then have the students go to four other students in the classroom, compliment each student, and write one student's name and the compliment given in each of the four stars. Ask the students to return to their seats. Instruct the students to complete their posters by writing the names of their remaining classmates in the small circles. When the students have finished, tell them to say, "I was kind to (STATE EACH OF THE FOUR NAMES WRITTEN IN THE STARS). Because of my kind actions, they were kind to others and (STATE THE EIGHT NAMES WRITTEN INSIDE THE SMALL CIRCLES WHICH HAVE ARROWS POINTING BACK TO THE LARGE CIRCLE) were kind to me.

- Conclude the lesson by telling the students that when students who tease want attention or recognition, receiving compliments may reduce their need to tease others. Suggest that the students try giving a compliment to someone who teases them and report their results to the group.

KINDNESS

GIVE COMPLIMENTS

SPREAD IT AROUND

41

LESSON 5
SEEING, SAYING, HEARING, REMEMBERING

Purpose:

To increase student awareness of differences in the ways events are heard, seen, and remembered.

Materials Needed:

For each student: None

For the leader: Copy of *Student Scripts* (page 44)

Activity:

The leader should:

- Tell the group that you are looking for volunteers. Each volunteer will stand in front of the group and be told about a brief incident. The volunteer's job is to remember as accurately as possible what he/she hears. The volunteer will then repeat what he/she has heard to the next person who enters the room. Remind the students that they will need to speak loudly enough so that the entire group can hear what they are saying.

- Select between three and five volunteers.

- Choose one volunteer to stand in front of the group. Have the other volunteers move out to the hall and stand there quietly. Remind the other students in the room not to laugh or giggle if someone makes a mistake. Explain that it is not easy to do this in front of a group.

- Read a script from the *Student Scripts* to the first volunteer.

- Direct the student closest to the door to ask the next volunteer to come to the front of the room. Then have the first volunteer repeat what he/she heard to the second volunteer as accurately as possible. Then have the third volunteer enter the room. Have the second volunteer repeat what he/she heard to the third volunteer as accurately as possible. Continue until each of the volunteers has had a turn to listen to the story and repeat it.

- Repeat the activity, using as many different scripts as time permits.

   Variation 1: Repeat the above activity with students individually viewing a picture and describing it instead of listening to a script.

   Variation 2: Have someone walk into the room to deliver a message. After the person has finished delivering the message, have each student write down what the messenger said and how he/she was dressed. When the students have finished, compare their answers to the correct responses.

- Ask the group, "What happened as the story was repeated?" Allow time for answers. (Usually the story becomes shorter, names are left out or changed, and the description of what happened may also change.) After the students have shared their accounts of what happened, ask, "Why do you think these changes occurred?" Allow time for answers. (If no one mentions it, tell the students that *what they think is important* and *their ability to remember* are the two factors that determine what they remember.)

- Suggest to the students that when teasing occurs, the parties involved may not agree about what has happened. Their perceptions may differ just as the volunteers' perceptions differed when they heard the story. Then ask, "What could you do to better understand others?" Allow time for responses.

- Conclude the lesson by telling the students that if they are teased, they might want to talk to the person who has been teasing them. If the person being teased shares his/her perceptions, and the person doing the teasing does the same, they might better understand one another.

STUDENT SCRIPTS

1. Rashad is a happy fourth grader. After school he decides to play soccer. While playing, he slips. When he gets up, a huge grass stain covers his right knee. He jogs to the restroom.

2. Carol picks up the phone and calls her friend, Olive. She asks, "Can you play after dinner?" Olive says, "No. I'm playing with Esmeralda tonight. We're playing hopscotch."

3. Carlos is working on his homework when Festus whispers the answer to him. Carlos doesn't believe that Festus is right. He asks his teacher, "Is 'B' the correct answer for number 12?"

4. Amoko is feeling sick. She asks Mrs. Broomfield if she can visit the nurse. Mrs. Broomfield asks, "Were you feeling sick this morning?" Amoko says, "Yes, but my mom told me to try coming to school."

LESSON 6
CONFRONTING A TEASER

Purpose:

To increase student awareness of how to talk about a situation involving teasing.

Materials Needed:

For each student: Copy of *Rules for Confrontation* (page 46)

For the leader: Copy of *Rules for Confrontation* (page 46)

Activity:

The leader should:

- Direct the students to divide into pairs. When they have done that, ask them to create a teasing situation and role-play it. Set a time limit for creating and practicing the role-play.

- Give each student a copy of *Rules for Confrontation*. Review the rules with the students.

- Ask for volunteers to perform their role-play in front of the class or group. If there are no volunteers, select a pair of students to perform the role-play.

- Ask the students, "If you were in this situation, how would you confront the teaser?" As responses are given, compare them with the *Rules for Confrontation* discussed earlier in the lesson. If some students respond in ways that are not covered in the *Rules for Confrontation,* discuss how their responses might lead to a change in behavior and end the teasing.

- Ask the person in each partnership who is being teased to confront the teaser according to the *Rules for Confrontation.*

- Conclude the lesson by asking the students to raise their hands if they believe they might use confrontation when they are being teased. Talk about why they think confrontation could help solve the problem.

RULES FOR CONFRONTATION

1 Choose a time when the teaser is alone and you think he/she might be in a pleasant mood.

2 Always approach the situation using a pleasant voice and polite words.

3 Start by suggesting that you might be at fault. For example, you might say, "I'm wondering if I may have done something to upset you?" or "Would you tell me what I did to make you tease me?"

4 If you don't get enough information from the teaser's response, ask if he/she can think of any way to solve the problem. For example, you might say, "Can you think of something I could do to stop this teasing?" or "Is there something you want me to do?"

5 If the teaser responds by suggesting something you could do or stop doing, consider trying that way of dealing with the teasing. If the teaser doesn't respond, you may suggest something. Make sure that whatever you suggest will benefit both of you.

6 Try to agree with the teaser on a solution.

7 If the teaser doesn't want to change, thank him/her for listening and move away.

LESSON 7
FRIEND/ENEMY

Purpose:

To provide students with practice in dealing with people who tease as potential friends.

Materials Needed:

For each student: Copy of *Friend/Enemy* worksheet (page 48), pencil

For the leader: Blindfold

Activity:

The leader should:

- Ask for two volunteers. Select two of the students who volunteer and blindfold one. Tell the volunteers that the object is for both of them to walk from the farthest corner of the room to the door without hitting or bumping into anything. They may talk to each other and touch each other as they proceed, but the blindfold may not be removed. Tell the volunteers to begin their walk. Tell the other students to watch them.

- Ask the group the following question:

   "Why were both volunteers able to reach the door?" (They worked together.)

- Give each student the *Friend/Enemy* worksheet and a pencil. Read the directions at the top of the page with the students. Then have the students complete their worksheets. Set a time limit for them to complete the activity.

- Have the students share their responses with the class or group.

- Ask the students the following question:

   "How does working with a friend help you deal with teasing?"

- Conclude the lesson by summarizing the students' responses.

FRIEND/ENEMY

Directions: For each situation, write down how you might act if the person doing the teasing was your enemy. Also write down how you might act if the person doing the teasing was your friend.

SITUATION 1: You're batting in a softball game. You swing at a pitch and miss. You hear someone tease, "You want my glasses?"

If the person were an enemy, I would: _____

_____

If the person were a friend, I would: _____

_____

SITUATION 2: You go to school with a new haircut. As you walk onto the playground, someone teases by saying, "What idiot cut your hair?"

If the person were an enemy, I would: _____

_____

If the person were a friend, I would: _____

_____

SITUATION 3: You just finished talking to Mrs. Galagos, the principal. Someone walks up to you and teases, "Tattletale! Tattletale!"

If the person were an enemy, I would: _____

_____

If the person were a friend, I would: _____

_____

SITUATION 4: You're talking with an older student. Someone pokes you in the side several times and rolls his/her eyes.

If the person were an enemy, I would: _____

_____

If the person were a friend, I would: _____

_____

LESSON 8
IGNORE

Purpose:

To provide students practice in ignoring teasing.

Materials Needed:

For each student: Copy of *Ignore Checklist* (page 50), copy of *Tease List* (page 51), pencil

For the leader: Copy of *Ignore Checklist* (page 50), copy of *Tease List* (page 51)

Activity:

The leader should:

- Give each student a copy of the *Ignore Checklist*. Review the checklist with the students.

- Ask for a volunteer to tease you about your clothes in front of the group. While the student teases you, you need to totally ignore what is being said. After a few minutes, ask the volunteer to complete the *Ignore Checklist* about how you did with his/her teasing.

- Give each student a *Tease List*. Review the list with the students.

- Ask the students to find someone with whom they have not worked before. Direct them to use the *Tease List* and take turns teasing and being teased. Remind the students who are being teased to ignore the other person. Allow each partnership to take several turns.

- Tell the students to complete the *Ignore Checklist* for their partners. Then have them share their completed lists with each other.

- Ask the students, "Is it easy to ignore teasing?" Allow time for answers. Answers will vary, but most students will find it quite difficult to ignore someone's teasing.

- Conclude the lesson by telling the students that if they are being teased and they believe the teaser is trying to control them, ignoring the teaser may frustrate him/her. In fact, ignoring the teasing may influence the teaser to give up trying to gain control.

IGNORE CHECKLIST

**To ignore someone's teasing means to act
as if the teaser were not present.**

It means you act as if nothing is happening.

**You don't change your facial expression and you
don't say or do anything differently.**

Directions: Place a (✓) check in front of each action performed
by the person you teased.

☐ 1. Facial expression remained the same.

☐ 2. Posture remained the same.

☐ 3. Person did not talk to me.

☐ 4. Person did not gesture to me.

☐ 5. Person did not make
eye contact with me.

☐ 6. Person continued to act
as if I were not there.

NAH! NAH! NAH!

TEASE LIST

Directions: When teasing, be sure to say the tease sarcastically. Repeat the statements as often as necessary to provoke a reaction from your partner.

1. "You're an idiot! You're an idiot! You're an idiot!..."

2. Point, twist your face, and shake your head disapprovingly.

3. "Hey, weirdo, where did you get those clothes? Rob a bum? Ha! Ha! Ha!"

4. "What's wrong, Chicken? What's wrong, Chicken?..."

5. "Look at the baby pout! The baby has to have his/her own way."

6. "You must be a freak. Only freaks do that!"

7. "Teacher's pet, teacher's pet, teacher's pet..."

8. "Nah! Nah! Nah! You run like a turtle..."

9. Rub your right index finger across your left index finger and say, "Shame, shame, shame!"

10. Point at the person and laugh as if there is something wrong with him/her.

LESSON 9
CHUCKLE

Purpose:

To teach students how to use humor to deal effectively with teasing and to give students practice in using humor to deal with teasing.

Materials Needed:

For each student: Copy of *Chuckle/Laugh* worksheet (page 53), pencil

For the leader: Copy of *Chuckle/Laugh* worksheet (page 53)

Activity:

- Ask for a volunteer to tease you. Tell the volunteer to say: "This is boring! Your class is boring!" When the volunteer says this, you reply, "You're right! You found me out."

- Discuss with the students how sometimes agreeing with the teaser in a joking way can help to eliminate teasing.

- Give each student a *Chuckle/Laugh* worksheet and a pencil. Ask the students to write a humorous response for each tease. Set a time limit for the activity.

- Read each tease description and ask for volunteers to share their humorous responses. Correct any inappropriate responses.

- Conclude the lesson by telling the students that joking can turn a hurtful situation into a comical one. You don't have to let anyone know you're hurt by the teasing. Accepting the tease in a humorous manner makes it easy for everyone to laugh and quickly move on to something new.

CHUCKLE/LAUGH

Directions: For each of the situations below, write a humorous response. Remember, an exaggerated or unlikely response made in a joking way is likely to cause laughter and deflect teasing. Be careful that your response does not increase the potential for conflict by making fun of another person. Also be careful that if you jokingly agree with the tease, your answer will not lead to additional teasing.

1. "Hey, toothpick, don't stand to close to the fan, you'll blow away!"

   _____

   _____

   _____

2. "Watch where you're going. What kind of an idiot are you?"

   _____

   _____

   _____

3. Someone's pointing at you, holding one hand over his/her mouth, and laughing at you.

   _____

   _____

   _____

4. You accidentally drop your books. Someone says sarcastically, "Hey, Klutz, get a basket!"

   _____

   _____

   _____

5. Someone picks up your pencil and holds it out in front of you. When you reach for the pencil, the person pulls it away. The same thing happens every time you reach for your pencil.

   _____

   _____

   _____

LESSON 10
CONTROL

Purpose:

To teach students different ways to control teasing and to practice these techniques.

Materials Needed:

For each student: Copy of *Basic Techniques* (page 55), copy of *Teasings* (page 56), pencil

For the leader: Copy of *Basic Techniques* (page 55), copy of *Teasings* (page 56)

Activity:

- Give each student a copy of *Basic Techniques*. Review the information with the class or group.

- Give each student a copy of *Teasings* and a pencil. Tell the students to write the technique they would use for each situation and explain the reason for their choice. Set a time limit for this activity.

- Read each tease aloud and allow students to share their responses.

- Conclude the lesson with a review of all of the techniques covered in the 10 lessons:

    – "I" Messages
    – Apologizing
    – Complimenting
    – Seeing, Saying, Hearing, Remembering
    – Confronting
    – Ignoring
    – Humor
    – Control

BASIC TECHNIQUES

1. **ASK THE TEASER TO STOP**

   Politely say to the person teasing, "Please stop teasing." Sometimes this is enough to end it.

2. **WALK AWAY**

   Walking away from the teasing will bring a stop to it. You gain control by no longer allowing the teaser to continue doing it. This technique is good when a teaser insists on teasing despite your polite attempts to get him/her to stop.

3. **SMILE/SHRUG YOUR SHOULDER**

   By smiling and shrugging your shoulders, you leave the impression that the teasing doesn't bother you. When a teaser realizes you're not going to react negatively to his/her action, the teasing will often stop.

4. **DO SOMETHING/JOIN OTHERS**

   A teaser will often pick on someone who is alone and not involved in an activity. By joining others, you make it more difficult for someone to tease you. If you're alone, the teaser has only to be concerned about your reaction. If you're with others, the teaser may be unsure of how your companions will feel and will not attempt the teasing. When you are with others, the teasing becomes more risky for the teaser. And if you are busy doing something, it's less than likely you'll notice the teaser and less likely that the teaser will notice you.

5. **CHANGE THE TOPIC**

   When someone is teasing, changing the conversation can stop the teasing. For example, if someone is teasing you about a mistake you made in a game, ask him/her about a recent movie, what he/she plans on doing for his/her report, or what's for lunch. Bringing something different into the conversation may move the focus away from you. It may stop the teasing.

6. **ASK OTHERS FOR HELP**

   Sometimes you may encounter a teaser who is very persistent. Despite your best efforts, the teasing continues. When this happens, remember that others can provide you with additional ideas to deal with the situation. The people who can help are classmates, neighbors, teachers, counselors, principals, parents, relatives, etc. Asking others for assistance may give you additional ideas and support to help you deal successfully with the teasing.

TEASINGS

Directions: In the spaces below, write down the technique you would use if you were being teased in the way described. Then write down why you would act that way.

1. **"Tattletale! Tattletale! You're always tattling to Mom!"**
   Technique: _____
   Reason: _____
   _____
   _____

2. **"You kick like an old lady."**
   Technique: _____
   Reason: _____
   _____
   _____

3. **Someone keeps pointing at you, twisting his/her face, and shaking his/her head up and down.**
   Technique: _____
   Reason: _____
   _____
   _____

4. **"Hey, Skinny, slide through that closed door."**
   Technique: _____
   Reason: _____
   _____
   _____

5. **"Where were you when brains were passed out?"**
   Technique: _____
   Reason: _____
   _____
   _____

SECTION 3
INDIVIDUAL PLANNING

DETERMINING THE PROBLEM

IDENTIFY THE PROBLEM

To successfully deal with teasing, it's important to know what the teaser does and how others respond to his/her actions. When you know these things, it is possible to take helpful action. For example, if the person being teased doesn't become annoyed, irritated, or uncomfortable, the teasing may stop.

There are two main ways to stop any teasing situation. First, the teaser can stop the annoying behavior. Second, the person being teased can change his/her actions. Since the person being teased has control only over him/herself, what this person does is very important.

FIND OUT ALL YOU CAN ABOUT THE TEASER

Before the person being teased attempts to do anything about the situation, it is necessary to look at the actions of both the teaser and the person being teased. *How Does the Teaser Act?* (page 60) reveals the teaser's actions. Completing this page will help you identify the teaser's actions and better understand the problem.

You may not always understand why you are being teased. In this case, you may have difficulty writing down specifics. If this happens, you should complete one or two *Teasing Observation Worksheets* (page 61). When you know exactly what the teaser is doing, it will be easier for you to decide on the actions you would like to take.

FIND OUT ALL YOU CAN ABOUT YOURSELF

The other area to examine is your actions. *How Do I React to Teasing?* (page 62) examines how you contribute to the problem. Completing this worksheet helps you better understand your behavior.

If you have difficulty admitting that you could be part of the problem, you or someone else may have to pay close attention to what you do. If someone else observes your behavior he/she should write down what is seen and then share it with you. This will help you understand what is really happening.

Completing pages 60-62 will help you to realize what is happening. Reviewing these completed pages will help you identify the problem. Knowing what the problem is, is important. It's the first step in planning a solution. If you fail to identify the problem correctly, you may do something that doesn't solve the problem or even makes things worse.

For example, if someone teases a student who wears green shoes to class each day, the problem could be what the person has chosen to wear. Knowing this, the person being teased may choose to solve the problem by simply changing shoes, if possible. On the other hand, if the teasing is being done because the teaser simply wants to make life difficult, changing shoes will not work. A different solution is needed. Knowing what the problem is helps determine the solution.

HOW DOES THE TEASER ACT?

Directions: Answer each item about what the teaser does when teasing you. Use as many facts as you can in your answers.

1. What does the teaser say? _____
    _____
    _____

2. How does the teaser look?
    Facial expression: _____
    Posture: _____

3. How does the teaser act?
    ☐ Stares at me
    ☐ Places his/her face close to mine
    ☐ Makes eye contact
    ☐ Stands over me
    ☐ Shouts
    ☐ Hits
    ☐ Points
    ☐ Grabs
    ☐ Moves behind me

4. Where does the teasing happen? _____
    _____

5. When does the teasing happen? _____

6. Who is there when the teasing takes place? _____
    _____
    _____

7. Does the teaser also do this to others? ☐ Yes ☐ No
    If yes, who else does he/she tease? _____
    _____

TEASING OBSERVATION WORKSHEET

Place _____

Date _____ Time _____

Describe what happened:

_____
_____
_____

Who was there?

_____
_____

Why do you think the teasing was done?

_____
_____
_____

TEASING OBSERVATION WORKSHEET

Place _____

Date _____ Time _____

Describe what happened:

_____
_____
_____

Who was there?

_____
_____

Why do you think the teasing was done?

_____
_____
_____

HOW DO I REACT TO TEASING?

Directions: Think about what you do when someone teases you. Then answer each of the questions below. In numbers 3 and 4, place a check (✓) next to the feelings and actions that apply to you. You may write other actions and feelings on the blank lines.

1. What do I say when I am teased?

    _____

    _____

    _____

2. How do I look when I am teased?

    Facial expression: _____

    Posture: _____

3. How do I act when I am teased?

    ☐ Look away   ☐ Fight
    ☐ Scream   ☐ Argue
    ☐ Whimper   ☐ Stay away from others
    ☐ Cry   ☐ _____
    ☐ Tattle   ☐ _____
    ☐ Mumble   ☐ _____

4. How do I feel when I am teased?

    ☐ Threatened   ☐ Afraid
    ☐ Harassed   ☐ Sad
    ☐ Frustrated   ☐ Angry
    ☐ Embarrassed   ☐ _____
    ☐ Helpless   ☐ _____
    ☐ Worried   ☐ _____

EXAMINING POSSIBILITIES

Once you have identified both the teaser's actions and your own, you can plan a course of action. You can decide what can be done. You can decide what actions are worth trying.

WHAT YOU CAN DO

To learn what you can do about teasing, read *What Can I Do About Teasing?* (page 65). After you finish this sheet complete *I Can Control* (page 66). By completing this worksheet and *What I Want to Do* (page 67), you will be able to examine what you would like to do.

The areas you have checked on *What I Want to Do* will help you decide what things to change. When you do this, rank the possible actions from most important to least important. Then choose only one or two of the possible actions. Choosing only one or two increases your chances of success.

MAKE A PLAN OF ACTION

In dealing with change, writing a plan is the first step. The *Action Planning* sheet (page 68) outlines the steps necessary for a plan of action. Read it carefully. Then complete your *Plan of Action* (page 69). The plan will help you focus your efforts towards effectively dealing with the teaser. It lists what you need to do and it reminds you of why you need to do it. If you need help deciding what to do when you are teased, look at the *Tease Solutions* (page 70). This is a list of actions you can take when someone teases you.

The second step is putting your plan into action. Believe that you will do well. Expect that you will do well. Do the things that you've written down. You may need to practice. Once you're comfortable with the action(s), use your plan when someone teases you. Do your best.

Examining your plan's effectiveness is the third step. This involves the follow-up part of the plan. You examine what's been done and what (if anything) needs to be adjusted to deal more successfully with the teasing. Many plans need to be adjusted simply because something unexpected occurs.

Be careful not to evaluate your plan before you have tried it several times. Sometimes a teaser has such a teasing habit that it may take several encounters before change occurs. You may still be acting as you did before making the plan. Habits are difficult to break.

SAMPLE PLAN OF ACTION

The problem is <u>Leisl covers her mouth and moves her mouth as if</u>
<u>she is laughing whenever I miss the ball in gym.</u>
_____

I will <u>not look at Leisl when I miss the ball in gym.</u>
_____

Good things that will happen if I am successful <u>I'll feel better.</u>
<u>Leisl will stop her silent laughing.</u>
_____

Bad things that will continue to happen if I'm not successful _____
<u>I'll feel terrible.</u>
<u>I'll be angry with Leisl.</u>

I will do my action by (DATE/DAY) <u>October 25—Tuesday</u>

FOLLOW-UP

REVIEW PLAN	DATE
<u>Tried not looking, but Leisl moved to where I saw</u> <u>her and she laughed. Decided to talk to her by</u> <u>Friday, Oct. 29. I will give her an "I" Message. I will</u> <u>say, "I get angry when you laugh at my misses in</u> <u>gym. Please stop."</u>	<u>10/26</u>
<u>It worked. Leisl didn't do it today.</u>	<u>10/29</u>

DON'T GIVE UP

If your plan does not bring you the results you want, don't hesitate to try something different. Keep trying. Persistence pays off. The *Tease Solutions* (page 70) provide additional ideas you can review and use.

Read and remember *Reaching My Goal* (page 71). This page is a helpful reminder of what you must do in order to achieve what you want.

WHAT CAN I DO ABOUT TEASING?

In answering this question, it is helpful to recognize what you can control and what you can't control. The following worksheets are designed to help you learn more about the kinds of things you can control. Knowing what they are will help you concentrate on what you can change to end the teasing.

For example, suppose someone is always teasing you after school when you walk by the library. Can you control the way you walk home? You probably can. By changing your route, the teasing may stop.

It is important to spend some time answering the questions on the *I Can Control* worksheet (page 66). After completing these questions, look at those to which you answered "yes." These questions show areas that you may be able to change. Knowing this will help you deal more successfully with teasing. By changing one or more of these areas, you may be able to stop the teasing.

Some of your answers may depend on where the teasing takes place. For example, if the teasing occurs in the classroom, it may be difficult to change where you are. You can't simply get up and leave. If it is occurring in your neighborhood, it may be very easy to move away from the teaser.

I CAN CONTROL

Directions: Place a check (✓) in the box in front of each item you can control.

☐ 1. I can control what I say.

☐ 2. I can control my facial expression.

☐ 3. I can control my posture.

☐ 4. I can control my actions.

☐ 5. I can control my feelings.

☐ 6. I can control what the teaser says.

☐ 7. I can control the teaser's facial expressions.

☐ 8. I can control the teaser's posture.

☐ 9. I can control the teaser's actions.

☐ 10. I can control where I am.

☐ 11. I can control whom I am with.

☐ 12. I can control the times at which I do things.

You will probably have checks (✓) in front of items 1-5 and 10-12. These are areas that most people can control. These areas usually are part of the solution to ending the teasing. The "yes" responses are your road map to changing your behavior.

Next, complete *What I Want to Do.* This will help you examine specific changes you may wish to make.

WHAT I WANT TO DO

Directions: Place a check (✓) in the box in front of each item you want to change. Write the change(s) you want to make on the lines below the item.

☐ 1. I can control what I say. I want to say:

    _____

    _____

☐ 2. I can control my facial expression. I want my facial expression to be:

    _____

    _____

☐ 3. I can control my posture. I want my posture to be:

    _____

☐ 4. I can control my actions. I want to:

    _____

    _____

☐ 5. I can control where I am. I want to be:

    _____

    _____

☐ 6. I can control whom I am with. I want to be with:

    _____

    _____

☐ 7. I can control when I do things. I want to do:

    _____

    _____

ACTION PLANNING

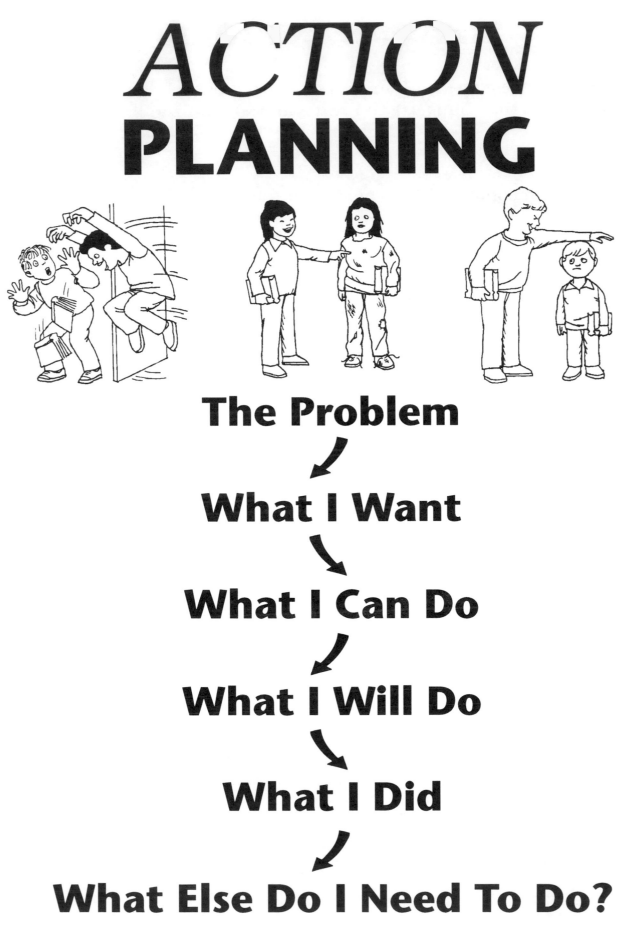

The Problem

What I Want

What I Can Do

What I Will Do

What I Did

What Else Do I Need To Do?

NAH! NAH! NAH!

PLAN OF ACTION

The problem is _____

_____

_____ .

I will _____

_____ .

Good things that will happen if I am successful _____

_____

_____

Bad things that will continue to happen if I'm not successful _____

_____

_____

I will put my plan into action by (DATE/DAY) _____ .

FOLLOW-UP

REVIEW PLAN   **DATE**

_____   _____

_____   _____

_____   _____

_____   _____

_____   _____

_____   _____

_____   _____

_____   _____

_____   _____

TEASE SOLUTIONS

WALK AWAY

UNDERSTAND THE TEASER'S REASONS

SMILE

GIVE COMPLIMENTS

SHRUG YOUR SHOULDERS

APOLOGIZE

DO SOMETHING

USE "I" MESSAGES

JOIN OTHERS

USE ASSERTIVE ACTIONS

CHANGE TOPIC

IGNORE

RESPOND AS A FRIEND

CONFRONT

CHUCKLE/LAUGH

ASK OTHERS FOR HELP

AGREE

ASK THE TEASER TO STOP

NAH! NAH! NAH!

REACHING MY GOAL

1. IMAGINE IT
2. EXPECT IT
3. PRACTICE IT
4. ACHIEVE IT

BIBLIOGRAPHY

Ballare, Antonia and Angelique Lampros. *Behavior Smart!* West Nyack, NY. The Center For Applied Research in Education, 1994.

Boehm, Ann and Richard A. Weinberg. *The Classroom Observer: Developing Observation Skills in Early Childhood Settings,* 2nd Ed. New York: Teachers College Press, 1987.

Bozzone, Meg A. "Spending Less Time Refereeing and More Time Teaching." *Instructor:* July/August 1994, pp 88-91.

Brigman, Greg and Barbara Early. *Group Counseling for School Counselors.* Portland, Maine. J: Weston Walch, 1991.

Campbell, Joan Daniels. "Soothing the Sting of Rejection." *Learning:* September, 1995, pp. 58-61.

Cieloha, Dan, Parker Page, and Mary Suid. *Getting Along.* Circle Pines, MN: American Guidance Services, 1990.

Collins, Dwane R. and Myrtle T. Collins. *Survival Kit For Teachers (And Parents).* Santa Monica, CA: Goodyear, 1975.

Cowan, David, Dianne Schilling, and Pat Schwallie-Giddis. *Counselor in the Classroom.* Spring Valley, CA: Innerchoice, 1993.

DeBruyn, Robert L. and Jack L. Larson. *You Can Handle Them All.* Manhattan, KS: The Master Teacher, 1984.

Feder-Feitel, Lisa. "Dealing with Violence." *Creative Classroom:* May/June 1995, pp 90-100.

Friedman, Alice and Fran Schmidt. *Creative Conflict Solving for Kids.* Miami: Grace Contrino Abrams Peace Education Foundation, 1985.

Garrity, Carla and William Porter. "Bully-Proofing Your School." Denver: Presentation at ADAD Conference, 1995.

Jones, Kenneth C., and Thomas D. Yawkey. *Caring: Activities to Teach the Young Child to Care for Others.* Englewood Cliffs, NJ: Prentice-Hall, 1982.

Kriedler, William J. "Nurture Kids' Instincts for Caring." *Instructor:* November/December 1994, p. 25.

Kriedler, William J. "Rid Your Classroom Of Put-Downs," *Instructor:* October 1994, pp. 28-29.

Krough, Suzanne Lowell and George M. Schuncke. *Helping Children Choose: Resources, Strategies, and Activities for Teachers of Young Children.* Glenview IL: Scott, Foresman and Company, 1983.

Millman, Howard L. and Charles E. Schaefer. *How to Help Children with Common Problems.* St. Louis: Mosby, 1981

Wilt, Joy. *Handling Your Ups and Downs.* Waco, TX: Word, 1979.

NAH! NAH! NAH!